1001 Email Closing & Valedictions

Flavio Olcese

Also by Flavio Olcese

Reyes Rising - Adventures of a Young Prodigy
Rebuilding Eden
Legendary Agent

Introduction

The truth is that writing "sincerely," as closing statement for a letter or email, just isn't sincere. It shows lack of emotion and imagination. This book was written for those who want to be more personal or original in their goodbyes.

Here is a list of 1001 letter and email closings that allow you to get your creativity going. Is this a complete list? Of course not, but from here you can launch into your own personal closings.

I have a friend who had a list of 50 or so closings that he used with his existing and prospective customers. He varied the ending with every letter. He told me of several new customers who called him to ask about the closings. He then had the opportunity to sell them his product.

Savvy business men make sales this way. Wait staff increase their tips by writing these on their checks. Friends get a smile and maybe a laugh from your thoughtfulness. And in case you don't want to be nice, we have included those truly awful closings too.

Read this book and highlight your favorites. Use them all the time. Go ahead and keep your friends, family and colleagues waiting for your next letter. Be fun, be mean, be silly and be original.

Confusion to our enemies,

Flavio

Contents

Formal & the Usual...............................Page 1

Love & Kisses......................................Page 3

Sweet & Warm Goodbyes.....................Page 5

Yours 'Til...Page 9

About Me...Page 10

About You..Page 14

Foreign Languages..............................Page 17

Funny & A Little Improper....................Page 20

Sports & Hobbies................................Page 25

Famous People, TV, Movies & Music........Page 26

God & The Monarchy...........................Page 28

Lust and Sexual Innuendos....................Page 30

Strange & Weird.................................Page 32

If You Didn't Get the Message Yet..........Page 33

Formal & The Usual

1. Goodbye,
2. Sincerely,
3. Most sincerely,
4. Yours sincerely,
5. Yours most sincerely,
6. Thank you,
7. Cordially,
8. Regards,
9. Kind regards,
10. Best regards,
11. Peacefully yours,
12. Very best regards,
13. Kind regards,
14. With kindest personal regards,
15. Salutations,
16. Truly,
17. Yours truly,
18. Respectfully,
19. Thank you,
20. Many thanks,
21. Thank you for your time and consideration,
22. Many thank yous,
23. Farewell,
24. Yours,
25. To you and yours,
26. Very truly yours,
27. Respectfully,
28. Yours respectfully,
29. Very truly yours,
30. Sincerely yours,
31. Best wishes,
32. Best regards,
33. Your colleague,
34. With confidence,
35. Wishing you the best,
36. Thank you for your kindness and consideration,
37. Until we meet again,

38. In gratitude,
39. Many thanks,
40. I await your reply,
41. In a cordial manner,
42. With fond thoughts,
43. In anticipation of your valued response
44. Thanking you in advance of your prompt attention to this request,

Love and Kisses

45. Adoringly yours,
46. Affectionately yours,
47. Always love,
48. As always, with affection,
49. Back at ya with the hugs,
50. Bubbles of love,
51. Caught up in the rapture of your love,
52. Forever yours,
53. French kisses,
54. Hopelessly in love,
55. Hugs and humus,
56. Hugs and kisses,
57. Hugs, Smooches and Nibbles,
58. I remain faithfully yours,
59. I remain lovingly yours,
60. I'm in love with you,
61. I'll be thinking of you,
62. In your arms soon,
63. Kiss you all over,
64. Kiss, you know where,
65. Kisses and cupcakes,
66. Kisses on those lips,
67. Kisses,
68. Living, breathing, loving you,
69. Loads of love,
70. LOL, (lots of love)
71. Lots of love to you and yours,
72. Lots of love,
73. Love always,
74. Love always, your sweetheart,
75. Love and lentils,
76. Love and lollies,
77. Love and taquitos,
78. Love with all my body and soul combined,
79. Love ya, Miss ya, Hug ya, Kiss ya,
80. Love you and now I'm leavin',

81. Love you madly. Need you badly. Miss you sadly,
82. Love you now and forever,
83. Love you so much,
84. Love you tons!
85. Love you,
86. Love,
87. Love, hug, and a kiss,
88. Love, hugs and kisses,
89. Love, hugs, and sloppy kisses,
90. Loves and hugs,
91. LUPR, (Love and unconditional personal regard)
92. Luv ya,
93. Luv,
94. LXLX ,(love and kisses)
95. LYLC, (love ya like crazy)
96. Miss you much,
97. Missing you with every breath,
98. Much love,
99. Muchas Smooches,
100. One love,
101. Peace & love,
102. S.W.A.K., (sealed with a kiss)
103. Smooches!
104. Sweet Kisses,
105. The heart knows no distance,
106. Til then, my beloved,
107. Tons of love,
108. Truly, madly, deeply,
109. Wanting you more,
110. With countless kisses,
111. With love as pure as the newly fallen snow,
112. With love,
113. With purest love,
114. With unstoppable kisses,
115. With vines of kisses,
116. XOXO, (hugs and kisses)
117. Yearning for you,
118. You are my heart,
119. You love me,

Sweet & Warm Goodbyes

120. Affectionate greeting,
121. All best wishes,
122. All best, always,
123. All the best for the rest,
124. All the best,
125. Always and forever,
126. Always in my thoughts,
127. Always true,
128. Always, forever, plus a day,
129. Anyones!
130. At your service,
131. Be good,
132. Be happy,
133. Be lucky,
134. Be nice,
135. Be safe, be healthy, be happy,
136. Be well,
137. Be with you soon,
138. Best wishes for your future,
139. Best,
140. BFF, (best friends forever)
141. BFN, (bye for now)
142. Blue Skies,
143. Bye for now,
144. Byes,
145. Call now,
146. catch ya later,
147. Catch ya on the flip side,
148. Check you later,
149. Cheers,
150. Come on home,
151. Drive safely,
152. Enjoy,
153. Enthusiastically,
154. Eternal,
155. Eternally yours,

156. Fair thee well,
157. Fair winds and following seas,
158. Fair winds to ye!
159. Farewell,
160. Fondly,
161. Forever and a day,
162. Forever and a day...or two,
163. Fortune everlasting,
164. Good wishes, always,
165. Grace and peace,
166. Happiness is a choice,
167. Have a great day/nite,
168. Have a great weekend,
169. Have a nice day,
170. Have a Purr-fect day, (cat lovers)
171. Have fun,
172. Health & happiness,
173. Here's to always having loving ways and perfect days,
174. Hope all is well,
175. Hope to hear from ya soon,
176. hope you have a super day,
177. In loving service,
178. In peace,
179. In solidarity,
180. It's been nice,
181. It's been really nice,
182. Just another day in Paradise,
183. Just to keep in touch with you,
184. keep in touch,
185. Keep it real,
186. Keep on keepin on,
187. Keep smiling,
188. Keep those cards and letters coming,
189. keep warm,
190. Keep well,
191. Keeping it real,
192. Kind thoughts,
193. Later,
194. Live easy, love freely, laugh loudly

195. Live well, laugh often and be merry,
196. Live well, laugh often, love much,
197. Live, laugh, love,
198. Love & light,
199. Love always,
200. Love your friend,
201. Love, luck, and lollipops!
202. many happy returns,
203. May blessings & smiles be yours,
204. May you have a smile on your face and a song in your heart,
205. More later,
206. Obligingly yours,
207. Onward and upward,
208. Over and out,
209. Peace and blessings,
210. Peace and long life,
211. Peace and progress,
212. Peace be with you,
213. Peace in the Middle East,
214. Peace,
215. Peace, love & happiness,
216. Peace, love and brown rice!
217. Peace, love and rock 'n roll,
218. Rejoice,
219. Rise and shine,
220. Safe traveling,
221. share and enjoy,
222. Shine on,
223. Short but sweet,
224. smile on,
225. Smiles and laughter,
226. Smiles,
227. So long,
228. SSS, (sorry so short)
229. stay in touch,
230. Stay well,
231. Strength, love and honor,
232. Sweet dreams,
233. Take care of yourselves…and each other,

234. Take care,
235. Take good care,
236. Take it easy,
237. Talk to me soon,
238. talk to you later,
239. Thank you for your undying support,
240. Thanks a million,
241. Thanks,
242. Thinking the best for you,
243. Till we meet again,
244. TTYL, (talk to you later)
245. unquestioningly,
246. until later,
247. Until next time,
248. Until next time,
249. Waiting,
250. Walk in light,
251. Warm best,
252. Warm regards,
253. Warmest greetings to all,
254. Warmest greetings to all,
255. WBS, (write back soon)
256. Wiggling my tail, (dog lovers)
257. Wishing you a safe journey,
258. Wishing you all the best of everything,
259. wishing you life's best,
260. With all best wishes,
261. with joy,
262. With kind affection,
263. With warmth,
264. Write back soon,
265. Ya all take care now,
266. Your friend,
267. Your pet,
268. Yours always,
269. Yours aye,
270. Yours ever,
271. Yours faithfully,
272. Yours,

Yours 'Til

273. Yours "til the road kills,
274. Yours "til the tie dies,
275. Yours 'til America drinks Canada Dry,
276. Yours 'til banana splits,
277. Yours 'til butter flies,
278. Yours 'til ice skates,
279. Yours 'til Niagara Falls,
280. Yours 'til the amusement parks,
281. Yours 'til the bug bites,
282. Yours 'til the candle sticks,
283. Yours 'til the chocolate chips,
284. Yours 'til the coco puffs,
285. Yours 'til the cow moooooooooooooss,
286. Yours 'til the crows fly and the flies crow,
287. Yours 'til the fat lady sings,
288. Yours 'til the goose bumps,
289. Yours 'til the Hersey's kiss,
290. Yours 'til the ice ages,
291. Yours 'til the kitchen sinks,
292. Yours 'til the lettuce peeks to see the salad dressing,
293. Yours 'til the penny drops,
294. Yours 'til the toilet bowls,
295. Yours 'til the world caves in,
296. Yours 'til your stars run out of time,
297. Yours' til turtle necks,

About Me

298. Affectionately,
299. Alive and kicking,
300. And now I'm tired, g'nite,
301. Anonymously,
302. As usual,
303. At you neighborhood, family friendly home depot,
304. Back to real world,
305. Back to the sweat shop,
306. Better than bubble wrap,
307. Boldly going nowhere,
308. Brazenly,
309. Bubblin' over,
310. Can't wait to see you,
311. Coming to a theatre near you,
312. Cry me a river,
313. Currently signed in....but signing out,
314. Dictated by me, recorded and sent by my really hot secretary,
315. Drunk and barely standing,
316. Especially yours,
317. Ever the same,
318. Fingers tapping,
319. From one loathsome smirking fiend to another,
320. From the mind of a genius,
321. Full of hot air,
322. Get me a Mars bar while you're out,
323. Gone,
324. Gonna fly now,
325. Gonna put an egg in my shoe and beat it,
326. Got to go, the office is on fire,
327. Gotta fly,
328. Gotta go, being shot at,
329. Gotta go, smells like poo,
330. Gotta make like a tree and leaf,
331. Help! Im on fire! Come put me out?
332. I am,

333. I better get off the toilet now,
334. I couldnt think of the proper closing to this email. I apologize,
335. I don't now what else to put,
336. I gotta jet,
337. I have to piss,
338. I hope to receive news from you soon,
339. I miss you more than I could know,
340. I puke for you,
341. I remain,
342. I rule you,
343. I think I might be sinking,
344. I worship you,
345. I'll lead, you follow,
346. I'm calling you, this typing sucks,
347. I'll keep you my dirty little secret,
348. I'm done, now you type,
349. I'm going where the water tastes like wine,
350. I'm gone,~poof!~
351. I'm gonna make like a baby and head out,
352. I'm outie,
353. I'm outta here,
354. I'm the best,
355. Impatiently awaiting your response,
356. In a drunken stupor,
357. In the hopes of shaking your tree,
358. Ink is low, gotta go,
359. Insincerely yours,
360. I've got your back,
361. I've seen that face before,
362. Just living and breathing and trying not to die again,
363. Just tryin' to stay one step ahead of the law,
364. Keep it between the white lines,
365. Kind regards,
366. Late is getting and I'm getting going,
367. LOL, (laughing out loud)
368. Love ya like a fat kid loves cake,
369. Makin' like Santa and leaving your presence,
370. Marking my spot,

371. Massively,
372. More meaningless drivel later,
373. My 5 mins are up,
374. My grandmother is on fire,
375. My imaginary friend says "hi",
376. My limo and jet are waiting for me,
377. My pleasure, always,
378. My time is up and I thank you for yours,
379. My, what a pleasure I am,
380. No longer yours,
381. Not from my blackberry,
382. Now don't say I never give you anything,
383. Off like a dirty shirt,
384. Off like a prom dress,
385. OMG I left the chip pan on,
386. OMG the dogs on fire,
387. Out like a fat kid in dodge ball,
388. Out like a trout,
389. Outta here,
390. Patiently awaiting your response,
391. Peas, I'm outta here,
392. Perpetually yours,
393. Playfully,
394. Prairie-doggin,
395. Progressively yours,
396. Regretting this already,
397. Remain with best regards,
398. Resting in peace,
399. ROFLOL, (rolling on floor, laughing out loud)
400. Serving wench, bring me my grog,
401. Shit, I left the stove on,
402. Shyly yours,
403. Signing off,
404. Silently,
405. Singing the blues,
406. Sorry I wrote,
407. Still crazy and lazy,
408. Still standing,
409. Streaking through the office,

410. Suspiciously,
411. Take me home,
412. Thanks for having pity on me last night,
413. That's me...(your name)
414. The one and only,
415. The pleasure is all mine,
416. This is my farewell to you,
417. Time to stretch,
418. Trashed and scattered,
419. Trudging the road of happy destiny,
420. Waiting for you,
421. Waving goodbye,
422. What was I talking about?
423. When you speak of me, speak well,
424. Whistling Dixie,
425. Will you still love me when you see what I have done,
426. With blood in my tears,
427. With crystal eyes and a heart of coal,
428. With trepidation,
429. With uncontained glee,
430. You're not the boss of me,
431. Yours in peace,
432. Can't think, brain numb. Inspiration won't come. Bad ink, worst pen. Best wishes, Amen!

About You

433. As you wish,
434. Back to you,
435. Be good. If you can't be good, be careful,
436. Be good. If you can't be good, don't get caught,
437. Be Splendid. Not Splenda!
438. Blog back!
439. Bring down the house,
440. Bring it on,
441. Call me or else,
442. Call me when you have money,
443. Call me when you're popular,
444. Carry on,
445. Catch you on the next bounce,
446. Did you fart?
447. Do the dishes,
448. Don't let your meat loaf,
449. Don't forget to breathe,
450. Don't forget to wipe,
451. Don't give up,
452. Don't let the bastards keep you down,
453. Don't look back,
454. Don't touch my tomatoes,
455. Follow your heart,
456. Get back here!
457. Get your dog off my leg,
458. Grab my knickers,
459. Groovy times for you and yours,
460. Happy Trails to you,
461. I'd say write me back, but you can't alliterate like I can,
462. I'll leave you to it,
463. It's not me, it's you,
464. Knit me a sweater,
465. Live on,
466. Look the other way,
467. Make me feel better,
468. Make your mark,

469. May fun characterize your evening,
470. May the four winds blow you safely home,
471. May you live in interesting times,
472. May you never thirst,
473. May your arrows fly straight and you aim be true,
474. Mind your manners,
475. Now go and get a real life,
476. Only you can prevent forest fires,
477. Pull it up to the bumper,
478. Remember what you're staring at is me,
479. Ride the lightning,
480. See you from the red carpet,
481. See you in the funny papers,
482. Seize the day,
483. Shake your booty,
484. Smell ya later,
485. Stand tall,
486. Stay as you are,
487. Stay beautiful,
488. Stay off the pipe, and don't forget to wipe,
489. Stay on the road 'cos its going somewhere nice,
490. Stay strange, don't be a stranger,
491. Stop sweatin' my diction,
492. Sunshine on you!
493. Tag you're it,
494. Take care, comb your hair,
495. Talk to my lawyer,
496. The pleasure's been all yours!
497. There's someone looking in through your window,
498. To you, the village idiot,
499. Wash your hands,
500. We're all fartin' for ya!
501. What's that behind you?
502. Who loves ya baby,
503. Worried about your mental health,
504. Still worried about your mental health,
505. Write when you find work,
506. You can do it,
507. You forgive me,

508. You lead, I'll follow,
509. You may already be a winner,
510. You rock,
511. You rub me right,
512. You still here?
513. You win,
514. You're not welcome here any more,
515. You're still reading this? The letter is over,
516. Your shoes are untied,
517. You're in my thoughts constantly,
518. You're killing me!
519. Yours smells,
520. You've been warned,
521. You've got mail,

Foreign Languages

522. À bientôt, (French, See you soon)
523. A toute a l'heure, (French, all has the hour, or anytime)
524. Adéu (French, goodbye)
525. Adeus, (Portuguese, goodbye)
526. Adieu, (French, goodbye)
527. Adiós (Spanish, To God, goodbye)
528. Adios amigo, (Spanish, goodbye friend)
529. Aishiteruyo, (Japanese, I love you)
530. Aloha, (Hawaiian, Hello/Goodbye)
531. Amicalement, (French, In friendship)
532. Amitiés, (French, Your friend)
533. Arrivederci (Italian, goodbye)
534. Au plaisir de vous revoir, (French, Hope to see you soon)
535. Au revoir (French, good bye)
536. Au revoir, (French, goodbye)
537. Auf Wiedersehen (German, goodbye)
538. Besos (Spanish, kisses)
539. Besos, mi amor (Spanish, kisses, my love)
540. Besotes, (Spanish, big kisses)
541. Bien à vous, (French, Yours truly)
542. Bien amicalement, (French, Yours warmly)
543. Bjocas, (Portuguese, short for beijocas, kisses)
544. Buenas noches (Spanish, good night)
545. Carpe cakem, (Latin-ish, seize the cake)
546. Carpe diem, (Latin, seize the day)
547. Cheerio, (English slang, goodbye)
548. Ci vediamo (Italian, see you)
549. Ciao (Italian, bye)
550. Ciao binky,
551. Ciao for now,
552. Ciao, baby
553. Con queso, (Spanish, with cheese)
554. Cordialement, (French, Cordially)
555. Dä ä görgött i skogera (Swedish, it's very nice in the forests)
556. D'ehre, (Austrian, sincerely)
557. Diolch yn fawr (Welsh, thanks)

558. Do svedaniya (Russian, until we meet)
559. Erromenon se hoi theoi diaphulattoien, (Greek, may the gods guard your well-being)
560. Fa Soifua (Samoan, take care, blessings)
561. Feri bhetaula (Nepali, we'll meet again)
562. Fica bem, (Portuguese, be well)
563. G'Day, (Australian English, slang)
564. G'Day, Mate (Australian English, slang)
565. Hasta luego (Spanish, see you later)
566. Hasta luego, (Spanish, until later)
567. Hasta luego, (Spanish, until later)
568. Hasta que los chismes nos separen (Spanish, until gossip do us part)
569. Hejdå (Swedish, bye)
570. Jag älskar dig (Swedish, I love you)
571. Living la vida loca, (Spanish, living the crazy life)
572. Mahalo, (Hawaiian, thank you)
573. Mahalo nui loa (Hawaiian, thank you very much)
574. Many mahalo's (Hawaiian, many thank yous)
575. Meilleures salutations, (French, warmest greetings)
576. Merci bien, (French, thanks very much)
577. Namaste (Indian Subcontinent, I bow to you)
578. Paalam (Filipino, goodbye)
579. Pax Vobiscum, (Latin, peace be with you)
580. Puss och kram (Swedish, kiss and hug)
581. Salut, (French, hello)
582. Salutations distinguées, (French, sincere greetings)
583. Sampai Jumpa (Indonesian, goodbye)
584. Saudades, (Portuguese, I´ll miss you or I miss you)
585. Sayonara, (Japanese, goodbye)
586. Sea feliz (Spanish, be happy)
587. Shalom (Hebrew, goodbye)
588. Slan (Irish Gaelic, goodbye)
589. Sliante (Scots Gaelic, goodbye)
590. Sov gott (Swedish, sleep tight)
591. Tanti saluti e baci (Italian, many goodbyes and kisses)
592. Te audire no possum. Musa sapientum fixa est in aure, (Latin, I can't hear what you're saying. I've got a banana in my ear)

593. TQM (Te quiero mucho, Spanish, I love you a lot)
594. Tschüs! (German, bye-bye)
595. Un abrazo! (Spanish, a hug)
596. Un beso, (Spanish, a kiss)
597. Veuillez agréer, Madame, Monsieur, l'expression de mes sentiments distingués. (French, Please receive, Madam, Sir, the expression of my distinguished sentiments.)
598. Veuillez recevoir, Monsieur, mes sincères salutations. (French, Please receive, Sir, my sincere salutations)
599. Vi ses (Swedish, see you)
600. Vsevo dobrovo (Russian, all the best)
601. Wo ai ni (Chinese, I love you)
602. Wo xiang ni (Chinese, I miss you)
603. Yn bur, (Welsh, yours sincerely)

Funny & A Little Improper

604. ....,
605. 45 calories in every bite,
606. A killer with the perfect weapons,
607. After a while crocodile,
608. All good, all the time,
609. All the news that fits,
610. Alrighty then,
611. Anyways,
612. As if,
613. Bartender's choice,
614. Be good or be good at it,
615. Be kind, rewind,
616. Bestest,
617. Bottoms up,
618. Breast Wishes, Sal & Manila
619. Bring on the dancin' boys,
620. Bubye,
621. Buenos nachos,
622. Buh-bye,
623. Bye bye custard and pie,
624. Can you dig it?
625. Catch you laterz,
626. Cheers & beers,
627. Cheers, big ears,
628. Chill,
629. Copyright 2008,
630. CUL8R,
631. Cya later mashed potata,
632. Destination unknown,
633. Don't come back now, ya hear?
634. Don't drop the soap,
635. Don't let the bed bugs bite,
636. Drive fast, take chances,
637. Dyslexics untie,
638. Ease on down the road of life,
639. Every man for himself,

640. Film at 11,
641. Find out next week,
642. Flying monkeys,
643. For the record,
644. From now on...
645. Further bulletins as events warrant,
646. Geronimo!
647. Gotta boogie,
648. Hails,
649. Happy end,
650. Hasta la bye-bye,
651. Hasta la Winnebego,
652. Have a decent day,
653. Have a funny day,
654. Have a very fruitful day,
655. Heads up!
656. Hell to the no,
657. Hello & goodbye,
658. Higher than an astronaut,
659. Hold please,
660. Holla back,
661. Holla,
662. Holy endings Batman,
663. Hoof hearted,
664. Horseshoes & hand grenades,
665. How come?
666. Hugs & Hersheys,
667. Hugs and pogo sticks!
668. In solidarity,
669. It's been real,
670. It's been real, it's been fun, but it ain't been real fun,
671. It's Great... but it's gettin' late,
672. It's now or never,
673. Keep in touch with yourself,
674. Keep on trucking,
675. Keep the pimp hand strong,
676. Keep the rubber side down,
677. Keep the shiny side up and the dirty side down,
678. Keep your shoes on,

679. Kisses and crossbones,
680. L8R H8R,
681. L8tr on,
682. Later gater,
683. Later skater,
684. Later tater,
685. Later Vader,
686. Later, chimp,
687. Laterz,
688. Let's go,
689. Like a withering rose,
690. Like it or not,
691. Lock & Load,
692. Love and anarchy,
693. Love and other indoor sports,
694. Made in Taiwan,
695. Make it snappy, nappy,
696. May the sale shoes always fit and never give you blisters,
697. Mind over matter,
698. Mix it up,
699. More rap later,
700. More shortly,
701. Musically yours,
702. My nigga,
703. Never sorry, ever jolly,
704. Never stop,
705. No funny stuff,
706. Not so fast!
707. Now we're straight,
708. Off like Tom Cruise,
709. On the rocks,
710. Out like the gay village,
711. Over,
712. Out,
713. Over & out,
714. Over the river and through the woods,
715. Pass the cheeze pleeze,
716. Peace and booty grease,
717. Peace out cub scout,

718. Peace out,
719. Peace out, home slice,
720. Peace, love & jelly babies,
721. Peace, love, and vitamin C,
722. Plant you now, dig you later,
723. Poof!
724. Power to the hippies,
725. Regretfully,
726. Right on,
727. Rock on,
728. Run for cover,
729. Run for your life!
730. Scratch and sniff,
731. See ya 'round like a donut,
732. See ya, wouldn't wanna be ya,
733. See you in the inbox kiddo,
734. See you later, sweet potater,
735. Send cash only,
736. Signing out,
737. Smell ya later,
738. Smoke 'em if you got 'em,
739. Soonishly,
740. Stay tuned, please...
741. Staying "in tune" with you,
742. Straight, no chaser,
743. Sucka what?
744. Surf it, don't dream it,
745. Thanks for all of the synergy,
746. That's the way the cookie crumbles,
747. That's all the news that is the news!
748. That's not funny at all,
749. That's the breaks,
750. That's the truth, no really!
751. The check is in the mail,
752. The End,
753. The stripper just got here,
754. The weather is here...Wish you where fine,
755. This can only end in tragedy,
756. Thoughtful giggles,

757. Till death do us part,
758. Till the bitter end,
759. Too bad, so sad,
760. Tune in next week. same Bat Time, same Bat Channel,
761. Visualize whirled peas,
762. Vive la revolution!
763. Void where prohibited,
764. WARNING: Virus Detected!
765. Watch this space,
766. We attack at dawn,
767. What's Neverland like?
768. With a song in my heart,
769. Word to the mothership,
770. Word to your mother,
771. Words aren't enough,
772. Y'all come back now, ya hear?
773. Y'all go straight home, now!
774. Yea OK, bye,
775. Yo Mamma,
776. Yours regardless,

Sports & Hobbies

777. Love-all, (tennis)
778. 1st and ten, (football)
779. Goooooooooooaaaaall, (Soccer)
780. 1st and goal, (football)
781. Till next time, (gardening)
782. Catcha later, (frisbee)
783. Buy for now, (shopping)
784. Love and cross-checks, (hockey)
785. Keep your stick on the ice, (hockey)
786. Swimmingly, (swimming)
787. Your hole in one, (golf)
788. Have a par-fect day! (golfing)
789. You are a real ace, (golfing)
790. Happy golfing, (golfing)
791. May the horse be with you, (equestrian)
792. May the wind always be at your back, (cycling/running)
793. Still pedaling your butt all over town? (cycling)
794. Ski you later, (skiing)
795. Feet passing in the night, (dancing)
796. Hugs and spins, (dancing)
797. Yours til the next dance, (dancing)
798. Dancing with gusto, (dancing)
799. May the god of dance smile upon your feet, (dancing)
800. Your dancing friend always, (dancing)
801. Yours in dance, (dancing)
802. Even when your imperfect, your perfect for me, (dancing)
803. I am, dear leader, your humble and obedient follower (except when I am not!), (dancing)

Famous People, TV, Movies & Music

804. All you need is love, (The Beatles)
805. Anything you can do, I can do better, (Annie Get Your Gun)
806. Be excellent to each other, (Bill & Ted's Excellent Adventure)
807. Carry on my wayward son, (Kansas)
808. Follow the yellow brick road, (The Wizard Of Oz)
809. Frankly my dear, I don't give a damn! (Gone with the Wind)
810. Go forth and multiply, (Star Trek)
811. Hasta la vista baby, (Terminator)
812. Here's lookin' at you, kid, (Casablanca)
813. I am the Walrus, (The Beatles)
814. I'll be back! (Terminator)
815. If you're caught or killed, the Secretary will disavow any knowledge of your actions, (Mission Impossible)
816. Just another loony off the path, (Pink Floyd)
817. Keep on rockin' in the free world, (Neil Young)
818. Laugh while you can, monkey boy, (Buckaroo Banzai)
819. Live long and prosper, (Star Trek)
820. Make it so #1, (Star trek Next Generation)
821. May the force be with you, (Star Wars)
822. My heart is ever at your service, (Shakespeare)
823. Never Mind the Bullocks, (The Sex Pistols)
824. Papa was a rolling stone, (The Temptations)
825. Put on your red shoes and dance the blues, (David Bowie)
826. Scooby Doobie doobie doooo, (Scooby Doo)
827. Screw you guys, I'm goin' home, (South Park)
828. Semper Fi, (US Marines)
829. Shine on, you crazy diamond, (Pink Floyd)
830. Snuffalufugus, (Sesame Street)
831. So long and thanks for all the fish, (Douglas Adams)
832. Solid, (Mod Squad)
833. Some girls give you children you never ask them for, (Rolling Stones)
834. Supercalifragilisticexpialidocious, (Mary Poppins)
835. Tartar sauce, (Sponge Bob)
836. These are not the droids you're looking for, (Star Wars)

837. Th-Th-That's All Folks!! (Porky Pig)
838. TTFN, (Tigger, ta ta for now)
839. Up, up, and away, (Superman)
840. We may have all come on different ships, but we're in the same boat now, (MLK)
841. Yabba Dabba Do! (Fred Flinstone)
842. You are the weakest link, (The Weakest Link)
843. You are young, and life is long, and there is time to kill today, (Pink Floyd)
844. You don't need to see my credentials, (Star Wars)

God & The Monarchy

845. 10-40 Lordy...over and out,
846. A demon with a smile of gold,
847. All I ask is that you treat me no differently than the Queen,
848. Amen,
849. Blessings,
850. From a humble slave to my Mistress/Master,
851. GLY&SDI - God loves you and so do I,
852. Go and make disciples,
853. Go with God,
854. God bless u, best for the rest,
855. God bless,
856. God save the queen,
857. God willin' and the creeks don't rise,
858. Godspeed,
859. Going to hell on the day that I die,
860. Greetings and salvations,
861. Holier than thou,
862. I have the honour to remain, Madam, Your Majesty's most humble and obedient servant,
863. If there's a heaven, I ain't going to it,
864. In God We Trust,
865. In His presence I remain,
866. In service to your crown and your kingdom,
867. In Spirit,
868. Keep the faith,
869. Kumbaya my lord,
870. Love in Christ,
871. May I always live to serve you and your crown,
872. May the gods have mercy on your soul,
873. May the gods not smite you,
874. May the gods smile down upon you,
875. Peace to your crown and your kingdom,
876. Prayerfully,
877. Seeking the holy grail,
878. Sin till we meet again,
879. Sleep in heavenly peace,

880. Smile, God loves you,
881. Spiritually yours,
882. The Queen is dead. Long live the Queen,
883. YHB, (Your Humble Servant)
884. YOB, (Your Obedient Servant)
885. Your loyal subject,
886. Your Majesties exiled servant,
887. Your master/mistress,
888. You're in my prayers,
889. Yours from the cross,

Lust & Sexual Innuendos

890. Beat me, bite me, make me feel cheap,
891. Big hug and an ass squeeze,
892. Can I touch your ass?
893. Can't wait to be with(in) you again,
894. Don't sweat the petty things, just pet the sweaty things,
895. Eat ya later,
896. Fuck you later,
897. Get laid,
898. Heywood Jarbloome,
899. Hoping you don't have tan lines,
900. Hugs and kisses and sexy wishes,
901. Hugs and kisses on all your pink parts,
902. Hugs and rug burns,
903. Hugs, kisses, and gropes,
904. I could eat you,
905. In loving mammary,
906. Kisses on the tip,
907. Later copulater,
908. Later masturbater,
909. Licking your chest,
910. Licks,
911. Longing for your touch,
912. Lovingly and lustily yours,
913. Lustfully yours,
914. May the seed of your loin be fruitful in the belly of your woman,
915. No pain, no pleasure,
916. Put your sexy hands on my rack,
917. Putting out,
918. Rock out with your cock out,
919. Slap my ass and call me Sally,
920. Smile, it's the second best thing your lips can do,
921. Sucking you dry,
922. Take it sleazy,
923. The fate of my girlie parts rests in your hands,

924. Time to get naked,
925. To my wit and your clit,
926. Wuv you...kissy, kissy (mmmm....and some touchy, touchy),
927. Your ass is mine,
928. Yours in abject lust,
929. Yours is bigger than mine,

Strange & Weird

930. 10 10 till I see you again,
931. A river dirty, (arrivederci)
932. Booyah!
933. Chow,
934. Coo coo cachoo,
935. fickle bickle, snikity snack,
936. Franks and Beans,
937. Funky chunky monkey out,
938. Geez lu-eez,
939. Hasta pasta,
940. Hooble-dooble doo!
941. huggy buggy.. Jumps on your back,
942. Kiss kiss bang bang,
943. Love & rockets,
944. Love, peace, and chicken grease,
945. Nickels & dimes,
946. Nickle pickle nicky poo,
947. Oky doky smoky!
948. Pickles and pimentos,
949. Respec',
950. Sha la-la-la-laaaa,
951. Shaboooom shaboooom,
952. Snapple, crackle, pop!
953. Sniffy lippy,
954. Someone get this freakin' duck away from me,
955. Squirrels and salamanders,
956. Tally ho,
957. Toodle-lay-dooooo,
958. Toodle-leigh-doooo!
959. Toodles,
960. Ur sazzy baby,
961. Uuuuummmmmm!!!!,
962. Whoop,
963. Wilen out,
964. Winner winner chicken dinner,
965. Yumpy chumpy,

If You Didn't Get The Message Yet...

966. ...and that's how I know you're gay,
967. Balls on chin,
968. Being a skank shouldn't be a family tradition, you cheap whore,
969. Bite me,
970. Ciao, you sick twisted fuck,
971. Curl up and die,
972. Flicking boogers,
973. Forever yours, ass monkey,
974. Go outside and play hide and go fuck yourself,
975. Hugs, kisses, and broken fingers,
976. I banged your mom, you illiterate cracker,
977. I don't like you,
978. I hope you choke,
979. I'd like to see things from your point of view but I can't seem to get my head that far up my ass,
980. If you were the last woman on earth, I'd fuck sheep,
981. I'm looking forward to the pleasure of your company since I haven't had it yet,
982. In a bit, chicken shit,
983. It's deep how shallow you are,
984. Let's play horse. I'll be the front end and you be yourself,
985. May the fleas of 10,000 camels nest in your armpits,
986. Note to self, I'm so glad you're fuckin' gone,
987. Piss n vinegar,
988. Quit being so stupid, you belligerent cunt licking buffoon,
989. Sleeping with your sister,
990. The divorce papers are in the mail,
991. The world is against you because you are a vindictive cerebral pus hole,
992. Thou art a gorbellied sheep-biting miscreant,
993. Up yours,
994. You can suck my mothafuckin' ass,
995. You is uglier than a lard bucket full of armpits,
996. You should come again when you can't stay longer,
997. You smell,

998. You will die alone, you phlegm covered genital wart,
999. You're a cold and unforgiving bitch,
1000.You're like a Slinky; not useful, but fun to push down the stairs,
1001.FUJIMO (Fuck U Jack, I'm Moving On)

www.ingramcontent.com/pod-product-compliance
Lightning Source LLC
Chambersburg PA
CBHW070844310526
45793CB00011B/530